Exploring Roots

by Kristin Sterling

first step nonfiction

Lerner Publications Company · Minneapolis

I see **roots**.

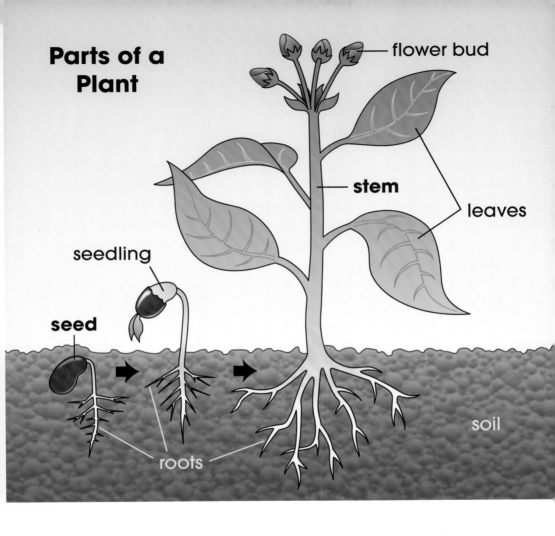

Parts of a Plant

flower bud

stem

leaves

seedling

seed

roots

soil

Roots are parts of plants.

3

Each plant part has a job.

Plants need roots to grow.

Roots grow down from a seed.

Roots keep plants in the
ground.

Roots help plants get water from the soil.

They send water to the
plant through a stem.

Some trees have big roots.

Most flowers have short roots.

Roots help these water lillies
stay in place in the water.

Desert plants store water in their roots.

People can eat roots!

Carrots and radishes are roots.

Roots are on your plate, in gardens, and all around you.

Do you see roots?

All Kinds of Roots

Big roots

Small roots

Roots that
hold up plants

Roots that store water

Roots that climb

Roots that people eat

Root Facts

 Food can be spiced up with the roots from the ginger plant.

 Water lilies float on top of the water. Their roots tie them to the bottom of lakes.

 Some root vegetables can grow in places that don't get a lot of sun.

 Roots are eaten by all kinds of animals. Elephants, wild boars, and porcupines eat roots.

 Carrots are roots packed with vitamins!

 Turnips are roots that don't mind being in the shade.

 Some swamp plants have roots that grow up into the air instead of down into the soil.

 Some roots have little hairs that take in water for plants.

Glossary

 desert – dry land that gets little rain

 roots – the parts of a plant that bring in water and keep a plant in the ground

 seed – the plant part that can make a new plant

 stem – the part of a plant that holds up the plant

Index

The images in this book are used with the permission of: © David Roth/Taxi/Getty Images, p. 2; ©Laura Westlund/Independent Picture Service, p. 3; © Cusp/SuperStock, p. 4; © Scott Sinklier/ AGStockUSA/Alamy, pp. 5, 6, 22 (third from top); © imagebroker.net/SuperStock, p. 7; © Jacques Jangoux/Photo Researchers, Inc., pp. 8, 22 (second from top); © Dennis Flaherty/Photographer's Choice/Getty Images, pp. 9, 22 (bottom); © pipdesigns/Alamy, pp. 10, 18 (top); © PhotoAlto/ SuperStock, p. 11; © Tatiana53/Shutterstock Images, pp. 12, 18 (bottom); © Dusty Pixel Photography/Flickr/Getty Images, pp. 13, 22 (top); © Food Collection/Photolibrary, p. 14; © Eri Morita/Riser/Getty Images, pp. 15, 19 (bottom); © I Love Images/SuperStock, p. 16; © Ariel Skelley/ Blend Images/Getty Images, p. 17; © Robert Houser/UpperCut Images/Alamy, p. 18 (middle); © luchschen/Shutterstock Images, p. 19 (top); © Zhu Difeng/Shutterstock Images, p. 19 (middle). Front Cover: © Tim Robberts/Stone/Getty Images.

Main body text set in ITC Avant Garde Gothic 21/25. Typeface provided by Adobe Systems.

Lerner Publications Company
A division of Lerner Publishing Group, Inc.
241 First Avenue North
Minneapolis, MN 55401 U.S.A.

Website address: www.lernerbooks.com

Library of Congress Cataloging-in-Publication Data

Sterling, Kristin.
    Exploring roots / by Kristin Sterling.
        p.   cm. — (First step nonfiction—Let's look at plants)
    Includes index.
    ISBN 978–0–7613–5781–0 (lib. bdg. : alk. paper)
    1. Roots (Botany)—Juvenile literature. 2. Plant anatomy—Juvenile literature. I. Title.
II. Series: First step nonfiction. Plant parts.
QK644.S74 2012
581.4'98—dc22   2010042988

Manufactured in the United States of America
1 – PC – 7/15/11